Approximately Paradise

UNIVERSITY OF CENTRAL FLORIDA
CONTEMPORARY POETRY SERIES

Florida A&M University, Tallahassee
Florida Atlantic University, Boca Raton
Florida Gulf Coast University, Ft. Myers
Florida International University, Miami
Florida State University, Tallahassee
University of Central Florida, Orlando
University of Florida, Gainesville
University of North Florida, Jacksonville
University of South Florida, Tampa
University of West Florida, Pensacola

Approximately

University Press of Florida · Gainesville · Tallahassee · Tampa · Boca Raton

Don Schofield

Paradise

PENSACOLA · ORLANDO · MIAMI · JACKSONVILLE · FT. MYERS

07 06 05 04 03 02   6 5 4 3 2 1

Schofield, Don.
Approximately paradise. / Don Schofield.
p.cm.— (Contemporary poetry series)
ISBN 0-8130-2460-9 (acid-free paper)—ISBN 0-8130-2461-7
(pbk. : acid-free paper)
I. Title. II. Contemporary poetry series (Orlando, Fla.)
PS3569.C52515 A87 2002
811'.54—DC21   2001054026

The University Press of Florida is the scholarly publishing
agency for the State University System of Florida, comprising
Florida A&M University, Florida Atlantic University, Florida
Gulf Coast University, Florida International University, Florida
State University, University of Central Florida, University of
Florida, University of North Florida, University of South
Florida, and University of West Florida.

University Press of Florida
15 Northwest 15th Street
Gainesville, FL 32611–2079
http://www.upf.com

For Harita
for what was

Contents

Acknowledgments

Some of these poems, occasionally in different versions, first appeared in the following journals and anthologies, to whose editors the author expresses his gratitude.

Abiko Quarterly (Japan): "Cities"; "Sacks of Flour."
The Antioch Review: "Callicles Puts a Head on the Argument."
Atlanta Review: "Teaching High School in Greece."
Birmingham Poetry Review: "Beirut Pastoral."
Gaia: "Dead Shepherd's Hut"; "Volcano."
Knowing Stones: Poems of Exotic Places (anthology): "Island Dance"; "I Don't Know the Local."
The Ledge: "Big Little"; "Hitching."
New England Review / Bread Loaf Quarterly: "Hagar in the Wilderness."
Nimrod: "Each of Us a Broken Tally"; "The Physics of Parting."
Paterson Literary Review: "Homage to the Wheels."
Pavement Saw: "Sentimental"; "Swaying Doors."
Peregrine: "4 A.M., Leaving Karpathos"; "The Lights of Famagusta."
Poetry Motel: "Polyphemos on His Veranda."
Red Dancefloor: "Mud and Marble"; "Sarcophagi with Glyphs."
Red Dirt: "Lazarus in Love."
River Styx: "Hometown Junkyard."
The Sacramento Anthology: 100 Poems: "Signs and Arrows."
The Salmon (Ireland): "Each of Us a Broken Tally."
Southeastern Review (Greece): "Approximately Paradise"; "Resident of the Old City."
Southern Poetry Review: "I Don't Know the Local"; "Sarcophagi with Glyphs"; "Drystone Wall."
2000: Here's to Humanity (anthology): "Angel."
Verse: "Spring Cleaning."
Verve: "Blue Pears."

The author also would like to thank Anhinga Press, the H. G. Roberts Foundation, the Poetry Center of Paterson, New Jersey, the *Southern California Anthology*, the *Atlanta Review*, and the Visiting Writers Program of the State University of New York at Farmingdale for the awards they have given to some of the poems in this collection; March Street Press for including several poems in a chapbook, *Of Dust*; the University of La Verne, Athens, for travel grants that helped in the completion of this book; and Dennis Schmitz, without whose guidance these poems would not have been possible.

Did we not launch you well
for home, or for whatever land you chose?

—*The Odyssey,* Book X

Islands

Teaching High School in Greece

I wear slacks every day, teach *Gatsby*
to a class of Yiannakis and Marias, write Emily's
slant truth on the board, check their spelling books
as they carve their desks
with words I can't understand. I tell them

Huck sails the Aegean
on a raft knotted by the
Hero himself. The black stacks of Corinth
remind him of home. Hester loves
the Parthenon, its broken columns with letters
she can touch. Emily circles the Tower of the Winds,
clicking snapshots. Walt hears wind in an Aleppo pine,
thinks North America bigger, greener—endless
next to this thin sighing. Yet he likes it here:
the sunglasses he bought, the postcard
of Diana striding legless.

Truth is, I walk and walk,
not knowing even the alphabet.
Alone at tavernas, I drink retsina late into the night,
but my eyes are wide: This is Greece, I'm here
in the fire of an idea, on a wave of fear and doubt. Figs

brush my cheek when I enter the hotel
where I've learned to keep my dream intact
though the bed in the room above thumps all night
and all morning buses wheeze, trucks
blast past my stop with icons of the Virgin
wired to their grills, motorcycles
race past me on the sidewalk, collect at the light.
From the heart of the traffic I always hear
someone calling: *Helen, Helen.*

Sometimes, when I lean to make a correction,
a young face with ancient eyes
stares back. I'm sure
the dead snake they put in my desk
fell from the Gorgon's head, that I saw
last Sunday, walking through the National Museum,
Emily and Walt holding hands,
leaning close to Persephone,
her smile simple and clear.

I Don't Know the Local

word for that ridge,
    these steppes,
        those tall

thin evergreens here
    and there across this valley,
        the flock of sparrows racing

as if to slam into
    a wall, veering
        at the last instant

up into the dusk sky;
    no name
        for the back-lit figs, the tufts

of dangling grass, this path I walk
    to town, so I veer
        inward

to flint emotions
    which also can't be named,
        syntax felt

as one lone tree
    turning its leaves against
        impending rain;

no story
    to distinguish me
        from the world I pass through:

white ridge of my mother's arms?
    deep ditch of my father's
        last look? stiff

tufts of a self
        I've lost? Am I
            this man passing on a donkey,

two cows with sloped backs
        behind him, one white
            as his scarf, the other

dirty brown like his pants? He waves.
        I grin and point to the sky,
            say the one word I know

too fast. I want to cover this valley
        with words he understands,
            but I can't even gesture clearly.

He points a thick finger
        down to the ground as his donkey
            brays its long

abrasive lament,
        then they turn to a field
            of scrub, the cows

following without being led,
        sparrows jabbering
            as they dive into some darkening

tree while I turn again
        to this unnamed path—all of us
            turning and turning

on local earth.

Hitching

This old man with a bundle of grass
   is light as a leaf, would blow
      into roadside scrub but for the young

men lifting him over the tailgate
   and once again we race
      up stepped slopes split

by ravines, rocks falling when we pass
   close to the edge. I bang
      the hard shoulder of a crone

surrounded by baskets of leeks, bags
   of nails, bolts of cloth,
      tins of olives and cheese—she glares,

another grins toothless, a third,
   the young woman behind me,
      offers the edge of the sheet she holds

against sun and dust—
   na párete, na párete—and refusal
      impossible for the foreigner

wedged between strange lives, strange
   consonants I voice
      to thank them. Their words

are soft sometimes, like fruit
   the old man points to
      as we pass some orchards—

elliés,
   akhláthia,
      amíghthala—and hard

as the thump against my ribs
telling me I'll always
be foreign.

Island Dance

Mardi Gras, Karpathos

An old man in black
leads the snaking dancers. Two steps up.
One back.
                    And the whole village follows. Three hours.
Four hours. Not you,
                    visitor, watcher,
with men at wine. Tired wives.
Children asleep across folding chairs.
Fluorescent lights.

Time was, the old man sings, *Zeus*
stepped with us, in the body of a bull. Muscles. Breath.
Danced into the knife. Left these steps and gold
coins on the virgins' necks, dowries worn
with downcast eyes. Two to front. One to back.

Thoughts descend. Five hours. Six.
To smoke and gilt. Where Snake
has wings hard round St. George.
Hammered blood in hammered dust.
Two steps up. One back.

                    —The young men
won't wait. Blast of flute.
No, sing the old, *No, not yet!*
                    They leap.
Slap boots. Slap thighs. *Opah!* then go
out from the train. Whirl the dancers past despair.
Make it clear. Snake is here!
                    Waking wives, children,
even you, eyes on fire as morning light
comes through fluorescent glare—

You're with them now, the whole island
swaying home at dawn,
arm in arm up whitewashed stairs.

Bee Box

Not much plot here.
Only the taverna. Late afternoon. Panayiotis
bringing in his new bee box.

What a choir of opinion as the men gather round,
whether to slide the top, nail it or put hinges;
how to string a panel: *Fix it from inside,* says Akis. *No,*
says Yiannis, *Tie it from outside, to cut the knot
and slide the comb free.*

                        You'd think the assembling of hives
was an ancient practice, but, *Listen now
to see.* And, *Fuck your Virgin!* And, *Akh,
by my Cross, you're wrong!* Where's the poet

to rise and say, *There are always hives in the fields,
some nailed, some wired, why argue? The queen
will get her honey, boxes or no. She's like*

*that woman we held in our youth,
the motion of her hips
pulling us ever deeper into memory, while the others
who held her once keep coming like drones
for a kiss, a caress, a brief touch
of thigh—ahhh,
what honey!*
                        —the poet a stranger
in the corner with the wives.
Let the men argue what angle
will entice the queen, her rhythm
is already at work, so *keipello*

is not a plastic for ice cream, but once again a chalice
offered to the goddess; even the bottom of this coffee cup
bears a message, as Cassandra knew. *And Odysseus?*

—That beyond the buzzing contours of desire
the story comes round to return and home
is always a surprise.

Sentimental

If I could sing like the *tsambouna* whines,
like these men at the tail end of a drunk,
making up the words as the song goes round the dock,
how Father's dying and Mother complains and a daughter's
      run off
to a stranger's bed; how the olives failed and the donkey
was hanged and the Datsun got stuck in a ditch,

I'd sing Patty's dog arched halfway
to death—two yelps, a rabbit kick, then one
faint groan. Sing red earth on white fur.
If I could dance off the grief
like Mikhalis here, arms spread, turning in silence,

I wouldn't feel like that fist they pulled from the harbor
      floor,
that torso hollowed thin as a shell,
head asleep two thousand years. *Your weakness
is too strong,* my first wife said when she left. *All you do
is want, want, want.* One by one

they toss their bottles into the sea and stumble off
into first light. On the stone path to my room,
the goat, the donkey, the bleating lamb
all feed on hungry grass
pressing through stone
for light and air.

Volcano

Left Athens,
 Patty glaring, me yelling
  inside: *can't speak, can't make the*

right gesture—
 came to this island that blew
  millennia ago, wedge

once whole. Gulls circle
 a serene landscape. Flowering nettles
  on the paths. Stone walls

angling to a calm expanse of sky
 or sea. You can't tell here
  rising and falling

when some emotion will flood you—whose anger
 carved these terraced slopes?
  Whose longing planted lemons? Whose grief

pulled up good water
 through his broken reflection?
  Some days you see the mouth

steaming in the bay, bargain a boat
 and lean over the rim:
  gush of sulfur

from the cracked core of this island
 seething, compelling
  you to return to whitewashed houses,

blue-domed sky, peace
 at the center of storm.
  It's not serenity

that sustains you,
　　but rage
　　　　at the center of peace.

The Physics of Parting

A moment ago I heard the fine
spatter of rain in the field behind me,
water rising, ready to sweep me away. Aristotle

taught wet and dry are absolute
opposites, *each on its way*
to its natural place. So why

do I see a row of poplars along a wall
when I turn, wind prying dry leaves
up and down the golden trunks,

and still the hiss of rain in my ears? I think of the spider
weaving that last night it was *our* bedroom,
rising and falling in moonlight,

not like us but Socrates,
who kept standing and sitting those last nights
in his cell, curious about his presence there—

due only to bones and joints
and flexible muscles? the words he uttered
explained just by laws of sound and hearing? I ask

what law for parting lovers,
one wet, one dry? Our wholeness
was never a burden—then it suddenly hardened

in opposite directions. The web snapped in my face
when I finally rose and left, descending
into chaos, but for the mind,

pure and alone, weaving depths
to heights, mind so pure it makes
wings of thick gossamer and lost

love: *rise, now rise.*

Archaeology

Rocky cliffs. A few
sparse pines. The sea
wide as waiting arms.
Yet those arms would pound these cliffs
as if to purge some deep hurt, wind rip
thorn-topped rock walls, rattling
upright slabs as if to blast open
this field. Mother,

the snakeskin I found
a ways back, the way it crumbled to my touch,
makes me think of you as I descend
this ravine, makes me kneel to finger
the earth for shards, remember
the world once whole.

You kicked me out, a boy of four
with only your story as recompense:
thirteenth child, huddled in the closet,
your lumbering father thumping the boys,
fondling the girls. In my version

I'm in there with you, muffling your sobs,
wiping your tears, stroking your tangled
hair as your brothers leave, sisters,
finally your mother

leaving you with his new wife
till you too fled, husband
to husband, easy to hate
each one, dream your whole shift
of a new cop or driver full of empty
sweet talk. I know each one

touched you with want till you sent him away.
Look how far I've come,

alone after so many lovers,
scraping the rocky earth for a glimpse
of painted breast, gentle curve
of knee—I'd assemble

your whole body out of shards,
hug you tight as you once
hugged me—
                        In my version
we're both a bundle of shards
rocking on the sea's constant motion
all the way back to the source.

Dead Shepherd's Hut

Sure, I can fix the broken door, clear the brush
out front, find a rope and bucket for the well,
a mattress for the iron bed in this hut
I've rented for next to nothing, but what about
his coat and crook still hanging by the mirror,
the photo of bare-breasted women
in white shorts and red boxing gloves
squared-off and whaling at each other?

I've come here, a tangle of desires,
more like the brambles I open the shutters to, the random
twisted olive trees up this valley kilometers from the road,
come to lose myself in the deep lull
of summer, to be less than smoke
curling from a lamp, nothing and nowhere. I like to think

he woke early, herded the huddled goats
up the ridge, that he knew each one by its bell,
that he's still sitting where pine cones
crack in late morning heat, the place
he slipped through to death. He's buried
on the opposite slope, in the one bare patch
among briars and burned grass—*beyond desire,*

I whisper to myself. But when I stand at his rusty basin,
see these women he gazed at every morning,
the smell of leather and sweat implied
by their gleaming shoulders and gloves, the ripple across
    one breast
where a punch just landed, the spectators cheering
from the darkness surrounding the ring, even the referee
smiling and pointing—I wonder

what he thinks of pleasure now
that he's gone to the source. Dead shepherd,
are you still hovering near your body, or here with me,
gazing at this primal destruction, resenting
even your own birth, that wound that bore you?
Or have you come back with some different knowledge—
taking down your coat and crook
then winking at me with the eyes of a goat, behind their
    bright slits
some truth I just can't see.

Carbon

on a bust of Yiannis Ritsos

The sculptor wanted to show your pride—
close-cropped beard, tilt of head,
coarse shirt of a worker—
a man of the people—

but your eyes look way
beyond this place, toward light
clear as bells
ringing in the square

where an empty chair
beside a window
reflecting an empty sea
is your poem for today.

⁓

I stood at the door of your red-tiled
house, looking at your features,
thinking of what I heard on the radio
the day you died: carbon,
radiating from collapsed galaxies,
is the one element necessary for life—
every cell in every living body
has a piece of dead star. Your bronze

face a dead star,
your images like carbon working
in our minds, enigmatic, essential:
Owl. Broom. Banging
shutter. Scrap of paper
drifting by—
your name on it?

~

As for the skin the sculptor
made it smooth yet rough,
unreal texture that would be skin
if skin were immortal. You

are looking back from death
at your tiny island ringed by crumbling walls,
mostly tourists walking the cobbled streets,
gazing at the sea
hung near yet far.

Can they feel your presence
in their own pulsing veins?
how each time you breathe
the sea moves?

Cove

Gulls swoop down from shadowed
mountains as you walk
for water. Waves lap at boats not yet
in light. Stones
sparkle on the beach. Morning

stretches to noon,
till nothing is hidden. Cliffs, dark and wet,
rise from the sea, pocked, scaled with salt.
Clumps of earth where nettles root.
Higher up, the walls begin, stones
piled and wedged, terrace upon terrace, every
few stones an upright
slab—three, four,
five feet high. Where the terraces end—
boulders, thorny scrub, cicadas
chirring in one tall cypress.

At dusk everything recedes. Shadows
stretch over rocky slopes,
walls the plated spine of a snake
coursing through yellow stubble, fodder
for skinny-legged, floppy-eared, golden-eyed
goats. One in the lane, udders full,
paws at a fig beyond her reach.

Night, in the crease between hills,
where the underground spring bubbles to the surface,
where lemons grow, cucumbers, tomatoes, melons—a
    pond
with bullfrogs bellowing. Ticks and fleas around the eyes
of a mule no one bothers to name. Small white houses
with uncut spikes on their roofs, rusty feelers
glowing in the moon. No one's here.

Hills, stones, paths—all sleep to the breathing
sea. A place, just a place:
no meaning, no wisdom, no secret loves
or unrevealed purpose. You
an absence.

Swaying Doors

Hard to be
this body, 43,
eyes weakening, lungs rasping
more and more. Yet the sea
wants it, calls it, laps at my feet. And there
drifting on the surface, stretched by waves in one direction,
rippling breeze in another—my body
reflected among bright shutters and doors,
piles of yellow nets, boats tugging
at their ropes. This body would float
shafts of summer light
those long boyhood days
in my room, windows and doors
closed and me under the bed, swaying with kelp,
a translucent blowfish expanding
and contracting, at play in the shadowy depths. Who'd
   have thought
I would go from those first yearnings
to this wind-scarred, sun-beaten
cove, alone and wanting to be.

                        Not that I haven't felt
the body's dips, swells, whole walls
of emotion crashing down, felt its real
translucence, swaying with a lover, lost
in our one current. Felt it
contract to its deepest zero
when love is gone. The mind now knows
nothing saves the body—not love, not words, not
   childhood's
musings, not solitude
here with these swaying doors. Let these timbers
drying in the sand prop up

all the summer windows—this body goes on
expanding and contracting in its currents,
and mind—*yes* and *no, no* and *yes*—
follows.

Spring Cleaning

Collecting the unwanted
worn out and broken this first
warm day of a late spring,
yard cluttered with almond blossoms,
I hear a loudspeaker blaring
up and down the streets—
Paliadzis, Paliadzis—his three-

wheeled truck loaded
with torn couches, legless chairs,
cracked urns and lamps,
stacks of clothes
in plastic bags, piled high
and swaying. My body

should be there too,
hauled to his shop on an upcrop
of stone behind a row of Piraeus apartments,
some narrow yard or basement with rusting
wash machines, stacked motors,
hollow casings of water-heaters
standing guard over the dusty shelves.

And if he hauled me off who'd notice
my absence? Who'd step into that warm
hollow, hear the hiss of me dissipating, even the memory
of me gone, the energy that was *me*
swirling in some larger pulse, some greater
breathing, cured of want at last,
body set in a place above desire—

Paliadzis, Paliadzis,

spewing out exhaust
as he trundles by.

Sarcophagi

4 A.M., Leaving Karpathos

It's shallow here. The ferry can't come any closer.
We go out to meet it with our bags of lemons,
suitcases tied with rope. All one load to Leftheris,
who at sixty drachs per head rows us out
to a pool of light adrift on the horizon.

Tied to the hull. Stairs lowered. Strong hands
reach down through the light,
pull our rocking bodies
up from folded nets where we wait.
Where to step? What to hold?
Then a voice from above, *One step and you're there.*

Hector found us a place in tourist class, space enough
to stretch out and sleep. I awoke much later
to laughing sailors, whining infants, glaring lights and
    bouzouki
music. Someone talking of Thebes, what remains of a
    tomb.
Someone pulling the portal curtain back and saying,

We're there.

Sarcophagi with Glyphs

. . . there are also sarcophagi shaped like human beings . . . .
—*Guide to the National Archaeological Museum, Istanbul*

Was this one tossed to the rocks
with the babies born lame,
brides who failed to bleed,
or one who watched it happen—
who can say? They had wars, they had hunts and the birds
were all caught, their heads hacked away. Who can say
what they say
these glyphs?

⁓

Upstairs was a picture of village women
piled in a pit, faces pale
as the dolls they once had,
the spots on their cheeks not rouge,
bruises where bullets punctured
the skin, their eyes on the sky
or the body above
or the grinning soldiers who shot them.

⁓

That was Lesbos. When I was there
the sheep one evening
grazed by my door. I heard them,
a tinkling euphony. The wall
where I leaned to listen
gave a little as I recalled
that flock in Cairo,
dirty white with a splotch of red
on their rumps, scuttling through noon traffic.
The shepherd spit as they passed,
our driver explaining red
means they're ready for slaughter.
Then the wall gave way:

~

What's become of this man?
He's glad in the dark though he plays with the light.
The stelae can't stop staring.
That he stays is their trance,
tracing glyphs in the light,
tracing our long
list of the guilty.

~

Now he sees:
We'll place his head on the block,
his ears to the mark, then poke
the ribs so his neck juts up
and the blade cuts clean.
The axe will still shine
and his ears
want a sound want a sound want a sound.

~

There's a pheasant on the corner of this sarcophagus,
a hunt on the back. Soon we all participate,
we who mate with a mask,
we who tear with a word then gawk,
we who marvel at the well executed.
So bring your flocks, your bright-feathered birds,
your reasons for staring into the dark.
Come look. Come tap at the glass.

Approximately Paradise

On Masaccio's wall
Adam and Eve
flee the Garden
in pain, in glottal remorse
for all they've lost.

Why wail in shock,
cover crotch
or breast? We're shaped
by want then dropped
from the branch. We eat
the apple again and again
to recall the soft hush in memory
which is us as we walked
the edge of a ridge
far from knowledge.

Stalled by doubt,
the glitter of loss,
the body's length
of bulge and dip,
we make up a garden—
the balls so soft
they must be fruit,
the labia warm
as sun-drenched moss.
The lively browns

of Masaccio's brush
are the range of wants
we recall or wish
we recalled as we stare
through locked glass.

We can't touch his fresco,
those leaves, their flesh,
only walk out ahead of them

into the warm Florentine afternoon,
go sip a coffee
below Ghiberti's
golden doors.

Hagar in the Wilderness

Let me not see the death of the child.
—*Genesis*

We kissed the icons and left. I carried the child,
bread, a bottle of water. Later
we drank from wells bitter with shards,
ate locusts and scorpions, glad to be gone.
What nations do I want? Only Abraham's
arms on nights the dogs come
to sniff the child. I think of my doll

with corn eyes, the one I rocked
when she was scared—
I built a fire, said a prayer
and pushed her in. She was heavy.
There was nothing more for her
I could do. Under this shrub
he'll stop his crying. The sand
will cover him and he'll be calm.

How the rocks grieve
is not clear, or why
the birds keep circling,
except to remind me the angel
promised Paran with me the queen. I lie
in the sabra and laugh: Come
my wild son, my archer,
this is Paran, we're a nation
of dust.

The Lights of Famagusta

Cyprus, 1980

Last night I saw my home—
the lights, the streets, the fields
of Famagusta. They took it all
and left us Larnaca, this camp
for refugees. I carry,
on nights I climb that hill,
only one dim candle
from the chapel of St. Lazarus I pass,
thinking of the night we fought
from its roof, of tanks in the grove
and faces the color of dust
as they fell
like pears . . .

Some nights as I watch
I hear a mother calling
her sons to bed, and memory calls
from that wall where I played in the shade.
I find that wall in any wall,
her words in any darkness,
all we said now said by others.
The man asleep in my bed is me, as I
am any man who waits for what grows
in the fields beyond his window.
What's left of the man

who wanted to be a tree: a pine
calling to no one
as he stared from sleep, his roots
deep in another life
where love flowed through his branches?

What branches? A man doesn't fall
like a pear. He falls
like a man, holding all he's lost, and so
loses nothing. The olive dark of his eyes
ripens to wonder at lights
like the lights last night as I stood
on that hill above Famagusta,
bewildered and ready to fall.

Resident of the Old City

I am not strong. I am faith holding on.
The stone gates I pass through
are thick centuries, the walls scaffolded
to an ancient sleep. This early
only monks pass by,
tall, gaunt Ethiopians
with black robes that flare
like wings as they turn a corner
and are gone. Long before the tourists,
pilgrims gather at the gates
like the dead would
if the dead could leave their long rows
on the hills above the city. They'll kneel
at the shrines like the old olive trees of Gethsemane
lean their gnarled trunks toward the sun,
still offering meager fruit like votives,
or tears,
or drops of blood.

Late afternoon I sit in doorways
with Arab hawkers
who deal in copper, spice, meat
and nuts, who don't know
their daughters have the dark eyes
of mosaics, don't see the Byzantine crosses
in the pocked walls where they play—
and remember as a child
how I kissed the Wailing Wall,
sang a prayer with bobbing head,
followed a line of dancers as they left
the square. The Wall led my joy.
And still the walls lead, past Veronica's veil,
past the painted alley where the Armenians live.

And music comes, tourist rock
or *muezzin* at prayer. The wind rattles

and the day fades, only the weightless
rush of dark remains, and a light
in one shop still open. *Come,*
the owner says, *Have tea. My wares
are yours,* as he draws a curtain open
to another at work in the dark. It's the dream
I see, the one that sustains me—
the hammer, the gold, time pounded
into eternity: Herod's throne and Mohammed's dome
amid the rugs, the plates, the flimsy shirts
and hukka smoke, the walls alive
with crosses, crescents and stars.

Lazarus in Love

Yesterday near the well I tried to tell her
how it was: like hanging from a limb,
about to fall. We were walking in the garden. I was saying
how my body lost its edges and I fell
through hands into memory, to where I was
a child chasing caravans—rattle of carts,
smell of spices and dung. I saw
gypsies and tiny dancing dogs,
young boys juggling apples. That memory gathers
even now as we walk past houses
and up toward terraces where vines
strung to the sunlight continue to lengthen.
Through the dazzle of ochre, green and white,
I cull shadows for what memory savors.

I have watched her on the terraces with a basket,
singing. There's a rhythm to the lemons as they fall.
Does it matter if I'm edgeless, if I dangle all hollow,
if my indelible breath gets tangled in the brambles?
When voices erode me to an echo off the canyon,
will it be love, her hands trying to pull me back
when all I want is to be the wall,
the shifting palm, to lower my head
and drift like sycamores in the buzz of locusts?
What is love when lethargy rolls over me,
warm and welling? Let it pull me to stasis. I'll follow
all the spores that collect in some wet shadow.
They blind me with their clarity,
the reds and yellows of the garden where nothing
happens but opening and falling and soaking
deep into darkness. I would lean into the well,
slowly let myself fall, but she'll point—she always does—
to the water that comes up bubbling.

Beirut Pastoral

When a man hath taken a new wife
he shall not go out to war . . .
but shall remain at home for one year . . . .

—*Deuteronomy*

All day the guns pound from the mountains.
When a shell hits the arbor shakes.
The sandbags fall unless we prop them up.
Here in Besaam's garden
my new father-in-law talks
of mists in the Bekaa Valley,
deep grass hiding the ruins.
Dust hangs in the failing light. Before eight
we go home past the searchlights.

And his words go with us through the rubble—
to be a weed in Baalbek, a stone piled
in that Roman library with field and sheep.
The Romans left that valley bitter, defeated,
to shepherds who now sit and smoke and follow
the trails of jets across the dusk sky.

Home is harsh lights, locked doors,
torn shutters, one room looking out
on an alley of burnt cars. My bride and I
leave our clothes behind the door and go into
that empty room. When the spotlights pass,
our bodies shine like toppled statues.

Sacks of Flour

She leads the donkey or the donkey
    leads her
up past goat turds to sage,
walls with small stones,
            heavy rock,
upright slabs
                like doors. She wants in

where snakes go in,
                    where they leave
skins the wind dries up and blows
away. *Scatter me slowly,*
    she says

or would if she weren't thinking of Manos,
how he held her close
at first. It happened quickly from then on.
        They had work to do.
Children came.
    Children grew
and she hardly knew them
    nor these others

who'll clamber into her lap
tonight—*Yiayiá,*
Yiayiá, where'd you go
today? Why'd you buy
so much flour? When the processions pass

beneath her kitchen window,
            coffins open,
    faces and hands of the dead
            covered with roses,

she thinks of pastries,
        glazed on top
        and inside

sweet cheese.

Drystone Wall

My arms ache.
I'm no good with these stones though you
know to alternate upright flats,

oblong chunks, small
swirls of quartz. You lower
a slab, force open

the earth, furious waves at the cliffs
below, this wall
the only peace between us.

We loved for a time,
I think as I hand you
one round as a head, stroke it

as if it were you in your distance.
You don't see me bend,
legs straight, face

almost touching
dry roots, loose husks
of wild barley—you're busy

fitting stones the size of my breasts,
chiseling the curves till they lock
lip to lip. You think

I still love your body
lowering to me like a warm slab.
I hate the weight and groans,

hair grinding in my face. All I want
is to dissolve like a pine
fallen to the earth, a thousand

mandibles carrying me
into tunnels and vaults.
But it's you who falls

to the bed beside me, lost
in yourself. You don't see
that place where the underground spring

once rushed to the surface, now a tuft
of dry grass surrounded
by rocks and scrub. I'll fade

to an anonymous mound
of stones, let you stack
what fits—

breasts with rounds,
thighs as supports,
head with face

turned to the sky. But where
will my sex fit?—not with flats
or rounds, can't stand by itself. Let it be

a nest in this wall,
bundle of straw, dry leaves,
the molted skin between us.

Eidothea Grieving

The Ancient of the Salt Sea . . .
Proteus of Egypt . . . is, they say, my father.
—*The Odyssey*, Book IV

The waves keep rolling
and I keep asking
that vague mound under blankets,
why lion, why falcon, why a towering flame?
Why all those years walking the beach,
following your tracks with the urge for *you,*
your touch, *your* solidness, *your* hand
firmly holding mine?
You were grass once.
From then on I treaded the fields carefully,
wondering what shapes I took
in Mother's womb—or was it yours?
Did I step from your ear, a girl already
asking questions? I thought I could have you
with words, Father. While you slept
I would spread feathers, fur or sand—whatever
was where your ear should be—and whisper,
Who are you? Who am I?
I would touch my hair, my breast,
and shiver at the thought
that I'm not me, I'm *you.* Seals clapped
each time you became a towering flame
for the crowds of locals and travelers who'd wrestle you
for the future. Even after you'd won
you'd go on changing—
from a bull laboring up a hill to a boulder
rolling through scrub to a flicker
of trout or a gull barely touching the waves,
each shape coming in a flash then lost
in a sea of shapes, like these questions

I can't help but ask—
surely if you're nothing fixed then you're all things,
a *trompe l'oeil* of everything, right?—
except a father to me. When I step outside
even the mountains look like waves
against a hard blue sky. The breeze laps
at the unsteady boards of this hut,
and inside, your shifting comes slower:
no fire, no tree, you're almost
solid as you lie curled up in your bed.
Or is your dying just another disguise,
that urgent expression a fish caught in the nets?
I stroke your hair—*your hair*—smell the sea
on your fading breath. Let me
be the one who finally pins you—here, now—
makes you give me in your dying
the answers you never gave me living.
Let me hold your body
to its final shape: the un-
recognizable figure of a man.

Polyphemos on His Veranda

My cave is whitewashed of course, blue logs
    for rafters,
fish drying on the sill. All of it
    leans toward the sea
that glitters a million gold eyes tonight. My eye

grazes like a goat on Orion, the Bear, the jeweled belt
    of the Huntress, the flight
from Cairo to Paris. Twin hearts—one loves, one yearns
    to devour—I'm the beast
best forgotten. I remember that braggart Nobody,

his comrades' voices like chirring cicadas. I should've
    wiped away some goat turds
for them to sit, should've shared my best wine. But, oh,
    his mates were tasty
as lamb on a stick. Thought he'd blinded me, but this eye's

resilient, can spot the Huntress at the far end
    of the cove
collecting what shines. Crones say her temple sank
    to the bottom of the bay
and it's true: sometimes the sea holds like a swirling

pane of glass. From my porch I can see
    clumps of algae
on toppled columns, a sandal poking from silt, terra-cotta
    votives still legible,
the broken pedestal of the oracle

now a nest of octopi staring back at me. Currents
    wash over those columns
like the *meltemi* scrapes this cove,
    pulls another brick
from my wall. I watch it sink to the bottom of the bay,

as if my heart—the one that loves—
    wants some current to lift it
smooth and gleaming, set it gently on the sand
    among nets, broken oars,
scattered ash and bone, for her to find.

Callicles Puts a Head on the Argument

. . . I should not like the argument
wandering about without a head; please then
[Callicles] go on a little longer,
and put a head on.

—Socrates

I say pleasure is its own reward.
Nothing to do with order or balance
as the Old Man would have it. It is daring to rise
to whatever might be gathering. Even anger.
That slap from a mistress may bring on
Father, dank with wine and hugs so fierce
they mesmerized. And such music in his voice
as he answered my questions, not like me
bewildered by the bodies of women in the *agorá*
pouring out their leeks and winter oranges.

The robber in the alley demanding money—
there's pleasure as he grabs it, and pleasure for the victim
in the stories he'll tell. In the howling of jackals,
the rueful laughter of hyenas,
all we mime in ecstasy.
Such pleasure advancing,
all the prophets cry out
for fiery inundations,
as if anything
could keep us from the sublime.

Give me shadows. Curtains. All morning
in the bath, masturbating to the scent of the woman
last night. Was there temperance in her moans, balance
in the reeds that dangled above us? First I kissed
that perfect crescent, that birthmark on her neck, then
    sliced it
free. They found her and blame me,

the rabble pounding at my shutters demanding justice.
There's no order to the Cosmos, Socrates,
only the confusion of arms and bellies
rising in the steam around me. I'll dry off

and go out to the mob,
thinking of the pleasure of the pyre that awaits me.
Socrates, I've pressed it in a scroll. I leave it here
for you: That little crescent. That moon
with hair.

Paradise (of Bronze Age Construction)

Stone lintel. Stone ceiling. Dirt roof.
Walls thick and sloped on this traditional Kea house
to keep in the cool air. Lizards
come in. Goats graze on the roof.
Stone fences all the way down to the sea, and beyond,
the blue cliffs of the next island rising above the mist.

Apollo dead. Socrates Christian.
So the hermit on the opposite slope would have it.
He gives me cigarettes, candied water, repeats
his story when I pass: *Steerage to America,*
cabby and cook and half of me missing, yearning
for home. Walking the path to town,

I liken my own desires to locusts. When I stop to listen,
the two or three become an entire slope. Listen more
and it's a whole island of scraping legs.
They are the voice of this landscape.
I am the silence.

When I lean into the cistern for water, my face
shines back. Steady reflection, as Mencius taught,
is the way to wisdom, though Hsun Tzu warned:
Morality must be hammered into place.

How would I have it?
Grass wreath on my head.
Arms loaded with early figs.
Body moving in the motion of a snake, the motion
of pleasure. All our lives
solid, consistent, of Bronze Age construction.

Signs and Arrows

Signs and Arrows

point to this exit, that
     lounge. A voice pages

names you don't know. A conveyer
     lifts your suitcase from a depth
          you're not allowed to enter.

In your passport the photo
     was taken before you left—
          who were you?

Who are you now? Down I-80
     the arrows lead to a skyline you know
          yet don't. The mall

where the airport limo leaves you
     is where you once dragged K Street,
          the fountain on 10th

where the all-night traffic turned
     to do the loop again. From the bus up Capital
          it's the elms you notice,

how they soften the grid of letters
     crossing numbers. At 55th
          you get out where the city's first McDonald's

still stands
     over a field once your domain:
          there were kingdoms in that empty lot,

Helen and Telemakhos, the slaughter of innocents
     when the bulldozers did their work. You walk
          quickly to your old

junior high—no clock, no tower, no
    brick promising forever—earth's
        trembling made them tear it down—

but the Temporaries
    are still up, painted
        and on the side of the block

where the playing field was.
    You loved to cross that field
        in fog, dew soaking

pantlegs and studded
    boots with taps that echoed down empty halls,
        vague bodies behind frosted glass—

late again! Up M to 56th,
    your own street stares past you,
        the locked gates and barred windows

not from your time, nor the scribbled PG&E
    arrows and numbers here and there
        at the edge of the sidewalk—

like marks archaeologists leave
    at digs—they point to your driveway
        where you lean with the pine on the front lawn

toward your house, so tiny now, overflowing
    with memories: your graduation photo
        over the TV, his hat

on a hook by the back door, the bed
    where you slept, where he died.
        Now you'd crowd into that bed

next to your father, run your fingers
    through his patches of hair,
        let your eyes drift like his,

wrist dangle from the mattress,
 fingers opening and closing,
  pointing to where? You're a ghost

in front of your own house.
 The one or two friends you could visit
  would look from their distance and ask

how is life over there?—later for that—for now
 you want to kill time like you did at nineteen
  at the old park still lined with shrubs.

Now the picnic tables are cement, new lights
 on the courts, old men
  still rolling *bocci* balls,

white house at the end of the one-way
 still there, but not the Pontiac
  you broke into—

it must be junk by now,
 that hat in the backseat
  boxed up in some attic. The owner

grabbed you from behind, punching and yelling,
 pulling at your hands to see
  who you were . . .

Who were you?

Hometown Junkyard

Beyond the crushed pickups and vans,
the stacks of grills, hoods, bumpers and doors,
stands a pile of back seats. Brush off
the glass, lie down on the rotted
tuck & roll, feel the pulse the others left,

thin Renee, struggling, clothes half-off,
or Bonnie hiding her nakedness as a cop thumped
the glass, demanding I.D. Stripped of love
we don't know who we are, only the day's events—
Belfast Bomb Kills Four—

as we taped newsprint to my Chevy's windows
in that park where lovers, bumper to bumper,
found privacy. Or we make up
a name, someone else to be or be with
as the night goes by. *Hi Lois,*

I'm Clark, I said to that hooker on Broadway.
Fuck, no more, she replied as she led me
down a row of curtained stalls. This her work,
wash my cock, rub it stiff, let it hook
her deep. Slow she pumped, then fast, her face

hovering with a terse grin. *Git your nut, Boy,*
finish now, as another pulled the curtain back.
Stall to stall we rose, we men,
left our body's print in the lumpy Simmons,
pulled on pants over slack legs and swayed

out into the alley. Grant the body
this moment, half-happy, before the twisted shapes
in a Belfast parking lot come back to mind. Be the glad
span of flesh at the edge of a roped-off
street, not the one slammed down by a pulsing

shard, that parking lot bomb another kind
of lust, where parts lie scattered
amid sirens, screams, eyes pleading
for reason. Stripped of love. Not knowing
who we are.

Angel

after a photograph by Donald McCullin

Six boys just turning the corner,
one playing the *oud,* one firing
his Kalashnikov, one twirling his scarf,
all of them laughing at the woman
face-up in the street. It's funny
how her arms flung straight out,
the sleeves of her robe trailing
in mud, look like wings.
With each bullet this angel
jumps a little.

Back in America,
thumbing through a book of photographs,
trying to fathom what impulse leads us to shoot
even angels and corpses, I was listening
to my old neighborhood,
heard nothing that helped.
Then the garden greyed over
with rain, the hissing of passing cars
pulled me toward sleep, so I lay down
on my childhood bed. Donnie
whistled in my dream—
*Come to the schoolyard,
there's a fight!*

      That boy's head
Donnie jerked back
and I slammed with my boot—
I woke wondering
at my own cruelty,
how we laughed and clambered
over a fence, forgetting those eyes

staring from the blacktop
where we left him. What lack
and illusion turned that to fun?

Last week,
riding to the Beirut airport,
I was astonished to see Howitzers
hidden in a schoolyard—Besaam
grabbed my finger—
Don't point! They'll think
you're shooting. You're only asking
for trouble. But now, awake,
I can't stop pointing—

at those guns,
at that boy on the blacktop,
at these ones emptying a rifle
into a dead woman,
toward laughter down the street
I only now barely hear . . .

Mud and Marble

It was sad passing through Fresno yesterday,
all the way from Athens to find a childhood home
with blistered clapboards, stacks of newspapers on the
    porch,
an old woman hating the work of moving. The back yard
was strangled with thistles. Pomegranate gone.
Profusion of green where the faucet dripped.

I found the corner where I once played in the mud,
where leaves hissed, butterflies trembled on my fingers,
mandibles opened and a hundred legs
scurried deep into darkness. Kneeling there

I thought of a woman I lived with. When she was 4,
Gamal Nasser ran all the Jews out of Egypt. She fled
with her family to Zurich, London, Milan
then Athens. *The circumference of tragedy is impersonal,*
    she said once,
but our sadness is our own, then described an Alexandria
of servants and china and cooling doorways.

We lived together—how long?—in a suburb
where Hadrian vacationed. Mt. Pendeli rises
above the peninsula there, trucks haul down
the same marble as the Parthenon's. Alexandria, Fresno—
what we had then we have now,
in the original scale of childhood. No hammer
can knock it to nothing.

                    So I think as I walk
the Santa Monica Boardwalk tonight, listening to waves
lap at the concrete pier. What sadness
does this Rastafarian pushing a rusting shopping cart
beside me own? He keeps tugging at my shirt sleeve,
asking for milk and a light.

Cities

Man is a creature who lives in a city.
—Aristotle

My brother tells me, flipping channels,
in Tokyo they don't trash
vending machines, or splash them with graffiti.

Machines have spirits, ancestors
selling baseball cards, condoms
and sandwiches. I tell him in Athens

wherever they dig for construction they find
antiquities: A splintered cornice. Shards
of a floor. A boy's head, the papers said,

with bronze curls. By law, work must stop
till experts come, sift the jumbled layers
of stone and dirt—so a subway

can't be built, nor skyscrapers,
nor underground parking. No time,
the builder usually

keeps digging. Huge metal claws
recently tore through fossils of pines,
a grove to Hyacinth Apollo,

archaeologists say, the name for the flower
there long before the god or the Greeks,
growing wild out of the mouths

of the original settlers—reminding my brother
that Mother called, says she's moving
her mobile home again, up north,

some town called Paradise.

Each of Us a Broken Tally

—Plato's *Symposium*

At Ephesus I saw stones—
fluted, inscribed, worn round
and anonymous, one pile the library,
another the baths, and beyond, a temple
for some forgotten remembrance.

And in Montana, again stones piled
at the bottom of a hill. We were friends
getting ready to go off once more—Doug
to Tucson, Jack to upstate New York,
Barry and Jill selling their farm
on the Rattlesnake for who

knows where. I asked about the mounds:
Jill explained how stones surface when combines
harvest the slopes of wheat. *We'll haul them off*
to some ravine, let the earth swallow them again.

Below us, the woman I was with back then
was waving. I used to wonder
how long we'd be together. I see her clearly,
even now, turning from the bottom of the slope
in a long, slow, upward arc
as I walk down.

Free

Gates Park, Sausalito

I didn't come to Sausalito for African slippers
or Chinese kites swimming in doorways,
though I too would swim in the slightest breeze

toward this fenced-in lot where a grey-haired hippie,
stuffed eagle on his shoulder, sings oldies.
I sing with him, the effort easy, as I'm wafted

stall to stall, past handmade jewelry, rainbow candles,
a strobe light working the painted faces. In '66,
first trip, I became the green of a pine

in Golden Gate Park, so tall
I had to measure myself against the bridge.
I took the bus up Lombard, ran

till I heard tugboats below, felt the haze
opening just for me, saw long red cables
rising out of the fog

like pines! I leaned way out
over the rail, ready to dive to the root
of all pines. What stopped me?

The foghorns call
as they did that day. Traffic drones
with purpose. Workmen paint and repaint

the girders. Was it the quotidian
that embraced me? Instinct or the pull
of fate that held me back? Imagination

truly afraid to leap
without the body as a net? Whatever it was
held me there. Suspended. In the foggy present,

now the past
that's past. The past still here
has been herded into this dirt lot

the other side of the bridge, where merchants
parade the remnants of the Sixties
beneath a dayglo sign, assuring us we're all

FREE.

Blue Pears

*Nevertheless I have somewhat against thee
because thou has left thy first love.*

—Revelation 2:4

You remember the smell of perfume
from your aunt's dresser, how we pulled out
the books, colored pears blue, apples green.
I recall the smell of buttermilk
in my foster father's beard,
puttied coins from his pockets, how you and I
hid under the bed
told secrets and touched each other
where they said not to.

Now, on the patio of your own big yard,
you tell me of the men you've loved,
how their bodies seem less beautiful
than one rippling deer in the orchard
below the family cabin,
where at sunset does ate the fallen

and bruised. You bring out your latest,
an abstract oil: *Summer Landscape.*
I think of our house back then:
Ceiling cracked. Wallpaper peeling.
Cooler dripping all summer.
Her anger. His laugh. The sound
of a slap—why do I remember all that?

You explain:
*Red blocks of paint are petals
folding outward, black is roots
reaching for the unknown.*

And the tinge of blue along the edge
is the ripeness surrounding our lives
as we hold to what we first knew
of pleasure, the seed

of all sorrow.

Low Tide, Mount Shasta

Two hummingbirds
hover at bluebells, dart off
in a blur of color,
then back,
faces smudged with pollen,
together yet not.

     ⌣

On peaceful days
the Aegean is smooth. Skiffs bob,
one next to the other, each tethered
to its own reflection. Chios
or Samos, I can't recall,
only a whole summer
like that, the sea a clarity
underneath our talk of separating.

     ⌣

This morning I took this trail
rising from the valley floor
to climb out of myself—
soft leaves and needles
underfoot, steep culvert
with water tumbling to a ravine,
yellow-green saplings
rising through a fallen pine,
then this clearing with
wildflowers, hummingbirds
moving forward and backward

     ⌣

with equal ease. I've stopped
in the middle of my life,
unable to go forward or backward,
up or down without her. The path
is dry on the surface,

cracks like veins that cave in
wherever I step.

~

Our first summer we climbed down
the same rocky slope each day,
air heavy with the incessant drone
of cicadas, to the same cove,
same low slung fig, same goat
grazing on heavy clumps of fruit.
She'd lightly kiss my neck, then down
to my chest-hairs, hovering,
eyes half-closed, then a full
kiss on the mouth as we coupled
again and again
right there in the sand.

~

Turning to descend
I think how snow blankets this slope
six months a year,
how her warmth
made a place each night
where I could nestle.

~

The Aegean
has no tides worth measuring.
Waves come,
shatter a harbor of boats,
then stay so calm
the clarity seems endless.

Knots

At dusk poplars stand, almost transparent
against the terraced hills. Cypresses bend
though there is no wind. The sea glints bright

and dark with the hammered surface of an icon. Forty
   now,
leaning from my balcony, I'm ready to leave this landscape,
these gnarled trunks, fresh nubs

of figs in July, the face I see
when I lean into the well:
silver hair, eyes back-lit and calm.

First bells of evening. Hooves
on the cobbled path. No one near me. No urge
a fierceness, just this dream drifting on a current,

my body the husk a cicada leaves,
the spirit elsewhere—there
where tips of pines flare up

in last light. Earth tilts
to its needs as darkness pours
down from the mountain behind me, covers poplars,

this balcony holding like a skiff in high
waves. I dream of returning to boyhood,
when I laughed in the streets with my Cherokee father,

slid down any banister into his arms,
chimed *me oh me* as I tied his hands
with knots he taught me, leaned in a doorway and laughed

at his anger when he couldn't break free—that boy
is the core of me, the most experienced me, the one
in control on nights there's no moon

and boats arc out across the bay,
leave lamps and drifting nets.
Fish rise from the depths on shafts of light and I

would rise too, pulling the boy with me.
Two or three lit houses on the bay
complete the constellation. Fluid sky,

solid water, lights above and below me,
this current I've been riding forty years
pulling me into the drifting stars,

then *me oh me* as the knots tighten.

Big Little

Dawn comes slowly to this departure lounge.
The slot machines are silent.

A worker cleans the wall-size window.
On the runway, lights go out, one by one.

Under the wing of a white
DC-10, a man inspects

the inner wall of a turbojet.
He's lucky to be alive,

the doctor said to my mother
40 years ago, not far from here.

Now the air conditioners rumble
to a start. Shops begin to open. A lone,

impatient gambler
lets a coin drop.

     ⌣

Born in 24-hour
neon, my firmament—
The Silver Dollar,
The Gold Nugget,
Harrah's, Harold's, The Horseshoe,
The Prima Donna. Under dancers

tall as buildings,
flashing their garters—
dice rolling,
aces showing, slots
pouring out silver coins.

Then the Original
Expulsion: The Biggest

Little Boy in the World
sent off to return
every summer on a bus,

leaving a sleeping father,
a wicked stepmother,

for Mother
in her trailer,
just home from work,
counting tips at the kitchen table,
giving me the short-stack
of silver dollars,
telling me to come to the casino
for dinner.

Who was this woman
who took me in
and sent me away
each summer?

Thin legs,
heavy breasts,
tired eyes—the source of love
in a yellow uniform?

Well here I am, suitcase in hand,
The Biggest Little Boy in the World
forever coming back to love.

      ∿

What did we miss, Larry,
never living together? Not your fist
slamming through the pasteboard wall of Mother's
bathroom, aimed at me, the visitor,
for tagging along. But there I was,
that same night
riding shotgun, trading insults
with a Firebird from Sparks when a bottle
smashed across our hood and we jumped out

swinging chains, animal-glad
as the other guys. The Beast of Love

compelled me to tackle one guy
twice my size so you could escape.
Bloody lip, bruised rib—
wounds I was proud of as the cops
frisked me hard in the crotch, cuffed me
and brought me in with a violence
akin to ours. In the glare of a holding cell
you put your bandaged arm
around me. I saw in your bruised face
Father's eyes, Mother's cheeks, my own
puffed mouth. Who were we really fighting
back then—ourselves in each other?
our parents, one dead by now,
the other helpless?

I'm asking, Brother,
from a life fractured by endless
battling, keeping me distant,
even from myself.

~

Red upholstered doors swing open
to ovens with gauges and knobs,
a row of spattering deep-fryers,
a dishwasher grinding out
steaming bowls and glasses,
loud pounding at a waist-high
chopping block, some chef
calling out, *More roquefort!*

And I, the Runner,
the one who brings what's wanted,
descend into the basement,
enter the tall refrigerators,
letting the chill work its way
over my sweaty chest,

poke my finger into a vat of butterscotch,
and think of the showgirls' legs
constantly moving under their table
at break, how Freddy,
the gay busboy in love with a chef,
cried in the elevator, *I wanted*
a lasting relationship,

watching my breath
hover in front of me,
almost solid, almost able
to be held.

⌣

Last night I walked downtown.
A warm July evening. The Riverside
boarded up, still advertising
Wedding Chapels. Rings. A Garden.
The neon Forty-Niner over The Nugget
no longer winking. The 12-ft. showgirl
with a foot missing. Whole letters
burnt out: *UCK!*
UCK!

        Who'll tell these newlyweds
rushing by in white sportcoat, yellow dress,
where the arrows lead—to great
caverns of decay—worn carpets,
frayed tables. Eyes
bright with possibilities, they don't see
the tired waitress, tired
dealer shuffling slowly, tired cards,
tired dice, tired sweepers. Pit boss
and streetwalker, tired.

        When they pause
from the action
to see their happy faces

in the mirrored panels above,
silent men with pale serious faces
look down from catwalks.
Walking and watching.
Guaranteeing the fun.

~

In the seats beside me, Debbie, 10, Lisa, 9.
They don't remember their parents' divorce,
only flying every summer to Reno,
then back to Farley, Minnesota. Belts on,
shoes off, they count their change and giggle.
Loss hasn't hit them: *Step* this. *Half* that.
Debbie is a little woman, in miniskirt, thin-
strap blouse, mascara. She pulls
at her skirt, holds the top of her blouse
against her chest. *We're used to the trip,*
know what food to order, to transfer at Denver.
Yeah, says Lisa, all girl,
with freckles, a pink lace dress,
And we got a guardian angel, pointing
down to the city all three of us were born in,
the shadow of a wing
passing over.

Gnat

Cheek pressed to cold glass you watch orchards pass,
oil rigs like big clanking locusts,
shops, a bank, a gas station, lawns and houses,
fields of hay then fields of hops,
then orchards again. You watch and watch
till your anger and hurt are threshed to dust
drifting toward a vanishing point
you can't quite see.

Mr. Orange gets in the way,
rickety stands with handpainted signs announcing
lemons, apples, avocados, strawberries—jets of water
stretch across the sky, smudgepots flame
in daylight, but your thoughts hunker down

to muddy water. At dusk
you watch insects rise toward passing beams
of light, surge of *yes* lifting from stagnant
pools, felt shimmer of wings
in a whorl of ecstasy—what dream keeps pulling
from caked oil, rotting treads, rags flung
to drainage sluices? Arms hung like tired wings,
hunched in a dark corner of the bus—

you're the boy-gnat stunned senseless
by yet another mother pushing you away. You wish
the woman across the aisle were your mother, and don't,
this pattern of uprooting not play, nor that voice
like no other: the clear, rich tone
of *her* beneath the rick-rattling layers
of memory; her warm, enveloping flow before
cord cut, face smashed to cold breast. The Greyhound

pulls into the terminal, rush of workers
hoisting squeegees, slack sponges, wiping away

the crust of bugs from windshield, bumper and grill.
Snaking hoses lowering from rafters.
Rucksacks, duffel bags, boxes and suitcases
tossed on a cart squealing all the way
to BAGGAGE. Now it's only you on the bus
and the driver telling you to get your things,
time to go. I know you'd rather
be tossed to the lost-and-found or scraped to oblivion

than walk into yet another waiting room,
hands deep in pockets, holding back the surge
of expectation. But this depot is for merging,
not just for pulling apart, so boy-gnat
be joy-gnat—let your arms like wings
flare up—it could be *her*
bathed in light
the other side of glass.

Homage to the Wheels

Just as if one night
you happen to enter
the city that reared you . . .
  —George Seferis

Laying down his journal, I think of his life.
    Exile and birth, he spoke of them as one. He escaped
with his parents to this city, where I too fled
    years later, from the opposite direction. In his time
whole empires collapsed, cities razed, his people

driven into the holds of ships, all they managed to save
    grabbed from their hands. My upheavals are nothing
next to his, yet I feel that emptiness he describes,
    that yearning for a past I had to escape. He saw,
when allowed to return as a diplomat, his living room
    collapsed,

front door now a garden gate, fountain crumbling,
    graffitied,
        thistles growing in the basin. I saw stacks of books on
            the porch,
yellowed newspapers, an old woman being wheeled by her
    daughter
        down the steps, pomegranate gone, pine and eucalyptus.
I too want to know *the mechanism of disaster.*

He went on to become Ambassador to England, won a
    Nobel. Was it worth it?
        When he died the crowds rioted as they carried his
            coffin through this city
never his, his body their symbol of outrage at the
    Colonels.

Exile and birth. In the town where he was born, on
    bank
and office walls, he saw portraits of the father

of that new country. Downriver from where she was born,
    my mother is dying matter-of-factly. I wonder at my
      world
where power changes hands with a smoothness he'd envy,
    yet I'm battered like him, broken by oppositions
personal, invisible, in the stretch of body on body, its
    ramifications.

The dust of events covers what we've lost. Wheels pass
    over.
    Something new will be ground, I should say, but I
      won't. This is praise
without hope of renewal, pause in awe of the paths
    we take. I fled my country and wound up not far
from the crossroads where Oedipus killed his father.

Those roads, like the roads of my childhood, are lined
    with eucalypti, olives, cypresses. Here and there
a patch of fur ground into the asphalt.
    The wheels grind.
It just happens.

My Neighbor's Brush

I

Climbing this rock
I carry my neighbor's brush
with long stiff bristles—

emblem of my presence on this island, desire
to help, to be with the locals whitewashing their chapel—
loose head rattling on its handle tall
as a man, pocked and gouged and so many
layers of white nothing could get them off,

or tall as a lanky boy
eager for a pat on the back,
job well done.

~

Son of driver carries it,
son of waitress, gambler, lumberjack,
abandoned son of priest and nun, angel
with glasses, wedged with all the other
First Communioners. Whose child am I

here in a country of strangers? Stavros
brings goatmilk every morning, Kyria Maria
eggs, and another I don't know,
when the moon is low and the wind has stopped, leaves
    squid
on my steps. The man who rows his boat
and helps his maimed wife step out
has a life more solid than mine. *A hundred years ago,* he
    says,
fewer houses and not so many boats,
but the stone walls and gardens were here, that row
of lemon trees, more threshing floors and more
rimathes, *songs from Homer*
and before: their words have changed
but not the music and not our stories
of a lost home.

~

At dusk sometimes,
in the glow of pines, soft brown hills
of barley, smooth roll of waves, America,
I miss the neon milkmaid above the corner dairy,
the car lot flashing *Nothing Down . . . Pay Later,*
smoldering leaves in the empty field
next door: California
those around me think exotic, can't imagine
why I left. America, tell me again, remind me
whose child I am—father a driver,
mother a gambler; no, mother a waitress, father a drunken
Cherokee; no, father a parish priest, Father What-the-Heck,
mother Our Lady of Sorrows.

~

Days here
are wedged stones, my memories
jumbled rocks where a wall once stood—oil derricks,
burning rice fields, houses with sloping lawns, an
    esplanade
with pines that towered to the boy at 4; at 16,
liquor stores with caged windows,
whores smiling and calling me Whitey,
juvie guards in their glassed-in room,
shouting through smoke-stained holes
Step back—behind the white line—now!—

                                        stones
that if piled right could make a home
of sorts, like the homes here,

    ~

so tell me—

    ~

The men pause at the top of the ridge,
point their brushes toward the mist
below, in their rush of consonants
one word I know: *kolpos,*
which means both *bay* and *breast.*

90

2

Seven brushes. Seven buckets. Six locals
mixing well water with quicklime,
laughing as they estimate
the monthly pay they'd get for this
if paid at all. A glass of wine
for the seventh, bearded foreigner
they set to work on the outside wall of the porch.

I dip my brush, swirl it around, swing it
up to the top of the wall, wind driving
beads of whitewash into my mouth and hair,
cries of a lamb from the village below
into my ear. I stroke each spot
several times and several times
stir the grains of earth, loose stems, winged
creatures drowned in white—What's it like

to drown in white, arms and legs
glommed immobile, lungs filled
with so much purity? Where the stucco ends,

bricks in rows, globs of mortar.
I paint these too, till my bucket is empty,
then climb to the porch, face and beard
splotched white, a prophet come in from the wilderness,
ready to fling this brush, this almost
perfect image of the soul, down at my neighbors' feet,
speak my message from the divine.

Yet I have no vision of the world to come
or its end. I could say my body fails while the spirit
    remains
elusive as air, that the gap between
one life and another never fills
except with loss, but I'm not sure. And even if I rattled off

each precise step to salvation,
they couldn't understand my language,

maybe a word or two.

3

Wade and I hitching to Sacramento, sharing
a beer and cigarette, no one stopping so we're sitting
in the weeds and he's going on—

You think 'cuz you white the world be white
or you gonna make it that way
with them scrawny fists, but shit,
ain't no one doin' good
'cept somethin's in it for him . . . I slap

whitewash on stones wedged
under bricks, spread it deep into crevices,
thinking how my neighbors paint their world
white, even weeds and dirt
at the base of this wall—

so, white my adolescent anger
rifling cubby holes, car to car, any suburb
south of town. I thought I was getting even,
grabbing coins, wallets, shotgun shells, bottled
holy water, pliers, flashcubes, snapshots—now I know
I was hoarding tokens of the love
I thought everyone else had, and credit cards
to charge the bitterness to them.

Now I'd empty my bucket
into the cracked core
of that anger, fill and empty it again,
till a river of white
would flow from there to here
and every parent, lover or friend
I've ever wronged
would float by—

I'd stroke each one.
Stroke and stroke.
Wade was right.

4

No candles, no votives, no psalters' stand, no curtained
door to the altar, all the icons carried out; now Stavros
on a chair paints the line that separates
heaven and earth. *Mea culpa, mea culpa, mea maxima
culpa,* I chanted as a boy on cold
weekday mornings, sure I was damned. But here
when I step out of the empty chapel
I'm blinded by white,
till I lean into the well,
see my dark face shining back. If I were Odysseus,

this bucket would be my shield, this brush
paint circles to let the gibbering shades
come forth: first my father
with hugs more substantial than when he was
alive, still saying *I can't, I can't,* Mother
at a distance with her contrapuntal *I won't.*

Then my companions in the children's home—
Wade, Luna, Santucci, Bill and Roy
Steele—all of us at attention as Mother Cordelia
slams our gritty palms with a belt,
no woman or man under that white habit, just rage
to make us bad boys pure. Nothing

stopped my desire when a hair slipped down
Sister Hermione's forehead; even now I'd stammer
if she called my name, as if I spoke
some alien tongue—and I do:
America, I anoint my face and arms in your names
that will never leave me—
Fresno, Reno,
Yosemite, Nippenowausee,
The Great Divide . . .

Blasted innocence kept me going
like a log hurtling down one of your flooded rivers.
Here where I've washed up, my flesh shines
in the incessant *meltemi.* I watch the crumbling
cliffs below and feel the despair
always there, watch the waves and feel love
come and go. Heaven, earth or underworld—
not much difference here. I drop the bucket
into the *pigi*—*spring* or *source,*
the word's the same—lift this brush
and drift toward home.

University of Central Florida
Contemporary Poetry Series

Mary Adams, *Epistles from the Planet Photosynthesis*
Diane Averill, *Branches Doubled Over with Fruit*
Tony Barnstone, *Impure*
Jennifer Bates, *The First Night Out of Eden*
George Bogin, *In a Surf of Strangers*
Van K. Brock, *The Hard Essential Landscape*
Jean Burden, *Taking Light from Each Other*
Lynn Butler, *Planting the Voice*
Cathleen Calbert, *Lessons in Space*
Daryl Ngee Chinn, *Soft Parts of the Back*
Robert Cooperman, *In the Household of Percy Bysshe Shelley*
Rebecca McClanahan Devet, *Mother Tongue*
Rebecca McClanahan Devet, *Mrs. Houdini*
Gerald Duff, *Calling Collect*
Malcolm Glass, *Bone Love*
Barbara L. Greenberg, *The Never-Not Sonnets*
Susan Hartman, *Dumb Show*
Lola Haskins, *Forty-four Ambitions for the Piano*
Lola Haskins, *Planting the Children*
William Hathaway, *Churlsgrace*
William Hathaway, *Looking into the Heart of Light*
Michael Hettich, *A Small Boat*
Ted Hirschfield, *Middle Mississippians: Encounters with the
    Prehistoric Amerindians*
Roald Hoffmann, *Gaps and Verges*
Roald Hoffmann, *The Metamict State*
Greg Johnson, *Aid and Comfort*
Markham Johnson, *Collecting the Light*
Hannah Kahn, *Time, Wait*
Sharon Kraus, *Strange Land*
Susan McCaslin, *Flying Wounded*
Michael McFee, *Plain Air*
Judy Rowe Michaels, *The Forest of Wild Hands*
Richard Michelson, *Tap Dancing for the Relatives*

Judith Minty, *Dancing the Fault*
David Posner, *The Sandpipers*
Nicholas Rinaldi, *We Have Lost Our Fathers*
CarolAnn Russell, *The Red Envelope*
Don Schofield, *Approximately Paradise*
Penelope Schott, *Penelope: The Story of the Half-Scalped Woman*
Robert Siegel, *In a Pig's Eye*
Edmund Skellings, *Face Value*
Edmund Skellings, *Heart Attacks*
Floyd Skloot, *Music Appreciation*
Ron Smith, *Running Again in Hollywood Cemetery*
Susan Snively, *The Undertow*
Katherine Soniat, *Cracking Eggs*
Don Stap, *Letter at the End of Winter*
Rawdon Tomlinson, *Deep Red*
Irene Willis, *They Tell Me You Danced*
Robley Wilson, *Everything Paid For*
John Woods, *Black Marigolds*

Born in Nevada and raised in California, Don Schofield has lived in Greece for the past twenty years, during which time he has traveled throughout the eastern Mediterranean and has taught creative writing, literature, and English as a second language at the University of La Verne, Athens. His poems, essays, reviews, and translations have appeared in numerous journals in the United States, Ireland, Japan, England, and Greece. *Of Dust,* a chapbook of his poems, was published in 1991.